Module 1
My Introduction to
Mary Magdalen & How She
Came into My Awareness

KIM CINTIO

BALBOA.PRESS
A DIVISION OF HAY HOUSE

Balboa Press books may be ordered through booksellers or by contacting:

Balboa Press
A Division of Hay House
1663 Liberty Drive
Bloomington, IN 47403
www.balboapress.com
844-682-1282

Because of the dynamic nature of the Internet, any web addresses or links contained in this book may have changed since publication and may no longer be valid. The views expressed in this work are solely those of the author and do not necessarily reflect the views of the publisher, and the publisher hereby disclaims any responsibility for them.

The author of this book does not dispense medical advice or prescribe the use of any technique as a form of treatment for physical, emotional, or medical problems without the advice of a physician, either directly or indirectly. The intent of the author is only to offer information of a general nature to help you in your quest for emotional and spiritual well-being. In the event you use any of the information in this book for yourself, which is your constitutional right, the author and the publisher assume no responsibility for your actions.

Any people depicted in stock imagery provided by Getty Images are models, and such images are being used for illustrative purposes only. Certain stock imagery © Getty Images.

Cover design by Saint Tone Productions.
Painting of Mary Magdalen by Kim Cintio

MaryMuntoldTRUEstory@gmail.com
Indivinetime.com

Print information available on the last page.

ISBN: 978-1-9822-7061-2 (sc)
ISBN: 978-1-9822-7062-9 (e)

Balboa Press rev. date: 09/23/2021

I dedicate this book and these teachings to every beautiful soul who has crossed my path. You have shared your message to me directly and indirectly. In turn, you gave me the drive to move forward on my journey to share the light.

To my mother, Sandra, for all your love and support throughout the years. Thank you for believing in me to make this all possible. My mom passed away prior to the completion of the book. She now watches over me and will see it all from a higher perspective.

I love you, Mom!

❧ Contents ❧

❧ Acknowledgments ❧

I am extremely grateful to have this opportunity to share "Mary's untold *true* story of her life *in her own words*". The bond we share is indescribable. Since learning that she shares my physical body, I have felt her every emotion while writing this book and her teachings. For this, I am eternally grateful. It has been my honor to share her untold story.

To my dear brother, Steve, and nephews, Michael and Scott, for your love and support during the process of writing this book.

Janie Boisclair, my special friend. Thank you for your kindness and expertise in helping me to edit and in sharing your knowledge to assist me in the making of this book with Mary's untold story and teachings.

I appreciate you!

ᴇᴠ Introduction ᴓ

I have been a psychic medium, known as a trance channel medium, a clairvoyant (psychic clear seeing), clairaudient (psychic clear hearing), claircognizance (psychic clear sense of knowing), clairsentient (psychic clear feeling; empathy), and clairalience (psychic clear smelling) most of my life. I am delighted to share with you the direct channeling I received from Mary Magdalen herself in the hopes that it will enlighten you as to the truths about her life that have *not been told to date.*

Mary asks that you read her story with an open heart and mind to allow her words to infiltrate your being and to allow you to immerse in her truth in *her own words.* You will not find any of this material in any other form of written history or literature of any type, including the Bible, gospels, etc.

My spiritual awakening began in 2006. However, this sacred activation brought so much clarity and awareness forward for me to really understand what was coming together for my future endeavors.

In 2016, while on a sacred journey in Sedona, Arizona, I had a miraculous activation take place while I walked the medicine wheel at Amitabha Stupa Peace Park. It was there in the medicine wheel I was spiritually greeted by five sacred elder ancestors of the land. When they approached me, they cleansed me with sage, also known as smudging, as I smelled it. (Burning sage is used to cleanse a person or space of negative energy, unwanted spirits, or stagnated energies. It is an ancient spiritual ritual and a Native American tradition.) They also blessed me speaking in a language that was foreign to me. It sounded like it was in tongues or chanting like. I immediately felt the love and blessing overwhelm me. A sense of greatness was happening. They then asked me to stand in each direction while they continued to cleanse and bless me.

After they finished, I realized that something of great magnitude had just taken place. I went into the middle of the medicine wheel, stood there, looked up at the heavens with my arms outstretched, and expressed my gratitude. It was at that time that one of the women in my group came by and took a picture of me. That night, when I went to sleep, I had a vivid dream. In the dream, I saw myself with my heart wide-open and sharing massive amounts of love to the masses, including all humanity, the animal and plant kingdoms, and the world.

As I sit here writing this, I feel such an immense amount of gratitude for this amazing journey I am on. It was from this moment forward that I realized what was coming forward for me.

Through my channeling experiences, I have learned of my closeness to Mary and how she has already influenced my life.

My hope for you is to find and understand not only the truth about her journey from her own words but also how her wisdom has changed your life.

✍ Chapter 1 ❧

My Introduction to Mary and How She Came into My Awareness

All italicized print is Mary channeled through Kim Cintio.

My awakening experience began in 2006. When I mention awakening experience, it means awakened into the spiritual realm: the other side of the veil spirits, crossed-over loved ones, angels, and so much more. I knew that there was much more to discover than my normal life. An eye-opening experience for sure.

In the early years, I sat in a psychic circle weekly for three years, very similar to the one I teach presently. We were learning who our spirit guides were in our inner band, meaning our personal spirit guides who incarnated with us in this life. I learned their roles, their personalities, their purposes, and why they chose to guide us in this lifetime as they assist souls on their paths or purposes. In the psychic circle, we learned how to connect with our spirit guides and practiced sharing messages from spirit, which I enjoyed immensely.

All our spirit guides choose us, and we make an agreement with them prior to our incarnation in each lifetime. Many of them have been guiding us for many lifetimes.

Mary Magdalen has been my spirit guide since birth. She was my doctor of chemistry guide, which is my healer guide. When I was having my awakening experience and learned she was my spirit guide, I was in disbelief. I had no idea what would be coming from all of this. I really did not know that much about her as I was raised Jewish and knew nothing about her life with Yeshua. I had not read the Bible.

Mary says half of the information mentioned in the Bible did not take place in her lifetime. Many of the quotes from the Bible, from my beloved Yeshua, were not spoken. The Bible was written several years after our lifetime by the church to gain control of the people in a patriarchal society.

As I evolved in consciousness and continued my connection and study, I learned more about my mission here. I have been guided and have traveled the world to walk in Mary's footsteps and have had miraculous experiences along the way. I have learned so much about her through her eyes and her life with Yeshua.

I now have another doctor of chemistry guide named *Joshua* as *Mary* has taken another position in my life. Mary and I share the same sacred heart, and what I mean by that is Mary and I share the same physical body. We are two souls in one body as she is always with me. Not incarnated but sharing my body. We have a personal relationship as she often shares information with me. She channels through me indirectly while I am having conversations with others. Many have said they see her face in mine. I am always caught by surprise when this happens.

Yes, she still assists other souls on their path of love and light. I asked Mary, "How does that come about?" as I was very curious and hoped to get an understanding of how that works on the other side.

She said if you picture yourself as one soul energy, as we are all energy, then imagine and see several different cyclones of energy spinning off the main one. These separate cyclones spin off to assist other souls simultaneously.

Oh, OK. I can see that as I now can comprehend how this all takes place. *She said they all do it—all meaning all the ascended masters.*

I have had numerous experiences with Mary, Yeshua, and many other highly evolved *Beings* of light. I will be sharing more.

A Personal Conversation with Mary Magdalen: Mary Speaks about Her Role on the Other Planes

Since the time I crossed over to the other side, I have discovered so much more about myself and how things really are. I realized that while I lived on the earth plane that everything is just a mere illusion. My sense of sight and feeling has heightened to a degree. I can see things with a much broader perspective now. My role here on the higher planes is to assist other souls to reach new levels of consciousness, to assist them to remember who they are, and to help them see things from a higher perspective.

Many souls I assist have had some type of connection with me in the past or in a previous lifetime.

You see, my children of the light, it is all written in your soul contract, and we here on this side must abide with what is written. (See page 9 about the soul contract.)

This stands true for all of your spirit guides, guardians, archangels, ascended masters, and teachers. You chose this before you incarnated on the earth plane. Every single one of you came here at this time with a very important mission, and I (We), your guides, are here to make sure everything goes according to the divine plan. This is why many of you have felt my presence in different ways.

Some of you feel that you and I are one. Yes, in so many words, we are. But not exactly as how you are interpreting it. Yes, my essence is carried in your DNA, but not my soul's self. I have not incarnated since my lifetime with Yeshua. We are living in such a monumental time in the history of the universe in which many of you came forward to be a part of.

Many of you have chosen to become part of the rising of the "divine feminine." I am here to assist you to step fully into that role—the role of the divine feminine counterpart of the Christ consciousness. Yeshua is assisting those of the "divine masculine" counterpart. For all to come together as one unit to practice Christ consciousness or unconditional love in all that you do. No judgment, no fear, only love. Yeshua, like me and the other masters of light, helps and assists others to bring forth many lessons that need to be addressed. We help you to see things from a higher and a *different perspective. Then once you understand what it is you are receiving, you can be that lighthouse for another soul who crosses your path. With an open heart, patience, and love, we can all become who we are and who we came here to be.*

Note: My Personal Perspective

The *soul contract* or *blueprint* is the contract in which you sit down with your spirit guides, guardians, and teachers before each incarnation. It is at that time to determine and plan the lessons (a.k.a. karma) that were not learned from previous lifetimes as it is carried over into your present lifetime. You see, when a particular lesson comes forward in life and it is not acted upon and healed with love and grace, it must be repeated. This is the role of your spirit guides as they must abide to what is written.

Do you know who your spirits guides are? Can you feel their presence with you? As a child, I knew and felt their presence. I always had a sense of something more, as I would always hear them speaking to me. I used to always say, "Every time I do not listen, I am always sorry." Now I did not know that much about them until my awakening experience in 2006. During that time, I took classes, read books, and listened to Hay House Radio to learn more about what was taking place in my life that I could not quite explain. Every time I mentioned it to my friends, they would roll their eyes at me as if I were crazy or something. At first, it was discouraging, but I soon learned and felt that I was thirsty to learn more. It was during the classes that I learned who my spirit guides were, including their names, their roles, and what lifetime I had with them. I now have a personal relationship with each one of them. Each of them has a role or specialty that they take very seriously. The more you work with them, the stronger the bond and connection will be. You can connect with yours through meditation, classes, mentorship, and other modalities.

I now live a spiritual life and do not believe in any type of religion, as I feel religion is man-made. I have felt this way since childhood. My connection with the Universe is a direct connection. Mary speaks clearly to me and through me daily.

Workbook Questions

Chapter 1

My Introduction to Mary and How
She Came into My Awareness

1. List all the ways you have felt Mary's presence around and with you.

_____

_____

_____

_____

_____

_____

_____

2. Explain in full detail how you have felt her love and guidance. How does Mary affect your life? Explain and share different ways.

_____

_____

_____

_____

_____

3. How has Mary helped you in your life?

_____

_____

_____

_____

_____

_____

℘

❧ Chapter 2 ❧

Mary Speaks about Her Youth and Meeting Yeshua

Greetings, my beloveds. This is Mary Magdalen. I want to share with you a little about myself and who I was in that lifetime.

When I was a young girl, I was boisterous and carefree. I was always one to speak up first and share my feelings and opinions. Many times, it was welcomed, and other times, it was not. I learned at an early age that sometimes it was better to keep things to myself. As I became older, I felt the need to be heard. At age twelve, I was sent to study with the secret sisterhood of initiates under the wings of Isis. I was trained in the secrets of Egypt in the Temple of Isis. It was there that I was being prepared as a high initiate for future events.

During my late teens, I fully understood who I was and what was expected of me. I spent many hours in meditation with other members of the Magdalens. You see, my children of the light, during those times, it was not acceptable for one to sit for hours and meditate. Most of the time, we would go to a nearby cave to practice our gifts and our connection to Source, God, Creator, Universe (however you call our creator) to be undisturbed for a period of time. I always knew that there was a bigger plan for me.

It wasn't until I met Yeshua that everything began to come into play and make sense for me. I knew in my heart that he was the one who was going to help me to grow and evolve on my soul's mission, not only spiritually but as my love, my partner, my life. You see, we were and still are twin flames. When our eyes met, I automatically knew he was the one. I felt every cell in my body light up. A feeling so intense it is even hard to describe. A twin flame is a soul that is a mirror reflection of oneself. This soul is the sacred divine feminine or masculine. You share the same divine mission. It's a soul partnership, so to speak.

Now you may have different ideas or views on a certain subject matter, and this takes place to show the other how to see things from a different perspective. Yeshua and I have had many discussions about things completely different from the other. There is not right or wrong, only experiencing things from a different view. I always felt fulfilled and loved during these times. It actually made me feel more empowered. I was able to share parts of myself more freely, as I knew my beloved was always near. Yeshua says he felt the same. A sense of inspiration shared from one another.

Note: My Personal Perspective

Are you familiar with this part of her story? Or have you heard a different version? Do you have questions about what you just read? Can you relate to anything in Mary's life?

I relate to this part of her story by recognizing that I walked a similar path. Through Mary's guidance, I realized that my youthful days were also filled with my having to contain my thoughts. I did not have a Yeshua to share information with. Instead, I shared my thoughts with my friends to gain perspective. They did not always agree with my thoughts, but they opened my eyes to other ideas. Now as an adult, I reach out directly to my guides and share my thoughts and questions with them. You will also be able to work with your guides in this manner once you start on your own spiritual path and recognize your guides.

How can you relate to this, and has it helped you to realize Mary's essence is within you?

Workbook Questions

❧ Chapter 2 ❧

Mary Speaks about Her Youth and Meeting Yeshua

1. How does Mary's upbringing relate to your life?

_____

_____

_____

_____

_____

_____

_____

2. Were you a boisterous child wanting to know anything and everything?

_____

_____

_____

_____

_____

_____

3. Did you have a vivid imagination growing up?

_____

_____

_____

_____

_____

_____

4. Did you have a sense of the greater picture once you understood who you are and what was expected of you?

_____

_____

_____

_____

_____

_____

_____

_____

❧ Chapter 3 ❧

Mary's Birthplace and the Magdalens

Greetings, my beloved children of the light. This is Mary Magdalen. I would like to share with you more information about who I am and where I am from. I was born in Israel in the town of Bethany. My parents' names were Mary of Magdala and Joseph of Arimathea. I had a younger brother named Lazarus and a younger sister, Martha.

During those times, there were many people named Miriam, Mariam, Marriam, and Mary. Some had repeated names, and some were named after a town or city or were simply, like now, named after a father, mother, brother, or deceased loved one. We did not put that much emphasis on names as my name was in the beginning Mary of Bethany. Being in the town we were residing, all the Magdalens were later named Magdala in Israel. My name Magdalen has changed to Magdalene over the years. It is time to go back to Magdalen *as it is originally spelled. I do believe now the world is ready for the truth.*

Now you may ask, "Who are the Magdalens?" Magdalen is the name given to a group of Essenes of the Jewish faith who studied and meditated in esoteric knowledge. Esoteric knowledge is what you call in your terms today metaphysical knowledge. Back then, and up to just recently, it was not accepted. It was considered forbidden and not accepted as anyone who practiced any type of connection of this nature was shunned in society. They did not understand anything that was different from their everyday practices; it was out of the norm, so to speak. So we had to practice our beliefs in hiding, going to nearby caves to meditate and practice ascension, ceremony, initiation, et cetera, and our connection to the Creator. My family and Yeshua's family were all Magdalens, and many others were as well.

Now I would like to elaborate a little more about me and my family and the Magdalens. We are all part of what you would call the great central sun. What I mean by that is we all come together at this time to be part of the bigger whole—the bigger picture, you can say. We have mentioned time and time again that it is so very important for all to be who you are. Follow your own feelings and your own soul's mission.

Yes, jealousy and intimidation can occur, but just know that when this does happen, stop, breathe, recenter, and come back to center. My dear children of the light, it is of the greatest importance to love and support one another. We did as a whole. When one did not quite understand, we often sat with one another and helped the other to allow the feelings of not being in alignment come up and release them out. This is what I am trying to get across to all of you. This is not a race of who is more gifted. We must, yes, stand in our own power, but we must love and support one another. If you do have disheartening feelings toward one, then allow it to come out and release and heal from it. Forgive yourself, and move forward. We do not and cannot allow any type of discord. We must all work together as one unit for the divine plan to go smoothly.

Yeshua and I are watching over all of you and assisting you on your journey. Many other Ascended Masters are as well. Please feel free to reach out to us if you feel stuck or blocked. You may even feel guided to a certain individual who can help you.

Please, my dear children of the light, seek help where you feel guided with what resonates with you.

Note: My Personal Perspective

I really enjoyed getting the details of Mary's life as it is not written in any other writings or literature. Learning how she grew up helped me to understand the preparation for the bigger divine plan. There have been many times in my own life when I have been guided to take a class and did not question it. An example of that would be a class I took on deep meditation that taught me how to transport my energy. That class came into my awareness and helped me in my own evolution of growth and expansion. When I look back at my corporate job in health care for thirty-eight years, I feel the preparation helped me to be more assertive and to represent myself in a more professional manner with my clients. The preparation also helps me with the medical intuitive work that I do, as I feel it prepared me for the greater plan.

Do you believe that you have been prepared for the bigger plan?

Workbook Questions

❧ Chapter 3 ❧

Mary's Birthplace and the Magdalens

1. How does Mary's life resonate with yours?

_____

_____

_____

_____

_____

_____

_____

_____

_____

2. Do your beliefs differ from your family's?

_____

_____

_____

_____

_____

_____

_____

3. Do you have a strong spiritual tribe?

_____

_____

_____

_____

_____

_____

_____

4. Explain how your tribe supports you and your growth.

_____

_____

_____

_____

_____

_____

5. Are you comfortable sharing your spiritual beliefs with others and staying heart centered?

_____

_____

_____

_____

_____

_____

§

If you do not currently have a tribe, you may want to assemble one for yourself and others for love and support.

Congratulations!

You have just completed module 1. To learn about Mary's untold *true* story and teachings, see the other modules that are available.

Module 2 - Mary Magdalen's Current Sacred Mission
Module 3 - Mary Magdalen's Relationship with Archangel Michael
Module 4 - Nontruths Told about Mary Magdalen

Learn more, shared in detail, in the book titled *The Untold True Story of Mary Magdalen in Her Own Words.*

Printed in the United States
by Baker & Taylor Publisher Services